SURVIVAL CHALLENGE

THIRSTY!

Could YOU find water in the world's wildest places?

STEPHANIE TURNBULL

A⁺

Smart Apple Media

Published by Smart Apple Media,
an imprint of Black Rabbit Books
P.O. Box 3263, Mankato, Minnesota, 56002
www.blackrabbitbooks.com

Designed and illustrated by Guy Callaby
Edited by Mary-Jane Wilkins

Cataloging-in-Publication Data is available from
the Library of Congress

ISBN 978-1-62588-218-9

Photo acknowledgements
t = top; c = center; b = bottom; r = right; l = left
folio image Olga Ryabtsova/Thinkstock; page 2t Pavelk, r Diana Taliun, b Tubol
Evgeniya/all Shutterstock; 3 ArtmannWitte/Thinkstock; 4t Galyna Andrushko,
b Chee-Onn Leong/both Thinkstock; 5 Maridav; 6t Mario7, b Nathan B Dappen;
7 Maridav; 8 slavapolo; 9 Thirteen; 10 Gleb Tarro; 11t EcoPrint, b Warren Goldswain;
12 Konrad Mostert; 13t nrt; 14t Maridav, b Vaclav Volrab; 15 Piyathep; 16t Jon Buder,
l konmesa; 17t Robyn Mackenzie, bl juniart, br beebrain; 18l Efired, r Mongolka;
19 Maksym Gorpenyuk; 20t Alena Brozova, b Timothy Epp/all Shutterstock;
23 Steven Stedman/Thinkstock
Cover t gresei, b falk/both Shutterstock

Printed in China

DAD0056
032014
9 8 7 6 5 4 3 2 1

CONTENTS

TAKE THE CHALLENGE 4

KNOW THE DANGERS

ACT FAST 8

FIND WATER

GET DIGGING 12

COLLECT WATER

LOOK FOR PLANTS

CLEAN WATER 18

FILTER WATER

GLOSSARY AND WEB SITES 22

INDEX 24

TAKE THE CHALLENGE

Imagine you're an intrepid explorer trekking across dusty desert, barren plains or craggy mountains.

The sun beats down mercilessly and the land shimmers in the heat as you trudge onward, sunburned, sweat-soaked, and exhausted.

4

Desperately thirsty, you take a swig of water from your bottle, then realize with a shock that it's nearly empty. The horrible truth sinks in: you could die out here in the wild.

Your challenge is to find water—fast. Can you do it?

KNOW THE DANGERS

You're in trouble. Humans can only survive three or four days without water—and even less in hot places. But stay calm! Read up on the facts first.

WATER SUPPLY

Your body needs water to work properly, so you must drink fluids regularly. You also lose water all the time, for example through breathing out, sweating and going to the toilet. If you don't keep a healthy water supply, you become **dehydrated**.

The more energetic you are, the more water you lose through sweat. Take it slow!

DANGER SIGNS

So how dehydrated are you? Let's find out.

With a full supply of about 88 pints (50 litres) of water your body functions well and you can think clearly.

Losing up to 7 pints (4 litres) makes you thirsty and a little sick.

Losing up to 14 pints (8 litres) means your mouth is dry and you have no energy.

Losing up to 26 pints (15 litres) leaves you dizzy, confused, and close to death.

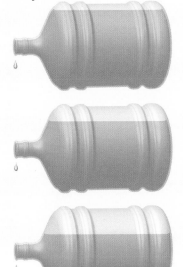

REAL LIFE SURVIVAL

In 1844, Charles Sturt set off from Adelaide to explore central Australia. He found a vast desert so fiercely hot that his thermometer burst. Soon he was dehydrated and starving, his skin sore and cracked from blowing sand. He just managed to struggle back to Adelaide!

HEAT EXHAUSTION

When you have heat exhaustion, your body temperature becomes so high that you sweat heavily and feel faint. It can lead to a serious condition called **heatstroke**. You begin to breathe fast, feel drowsy, and may collapse.

ACT FAST

You're mildly dehydrated and perhaps have heat exhaustion too. What should you do? Get out of the sun—NOW.

FIND SHADE

Look for shady spots such as rocky outcrops or caves. Trees and bushes may cast shadows big enough to crouch in. If all else fails, use a blanket or clothing from your backpack as a makeshift tent.

Cool, shady caves make ideal shelters. Just make sure they don't belong to wild animals!

STOP MOVING

Now rest. The less you move, the less you'll sweat. Try breathing through your nose instead of your mouth to lose less water. If you have spare water, wet a towel or T-shirt and lay it on your forehead, neck or wrists.

↻ *Lie down and try to relax to help bring down your body temperature.*

SIP A DRINK

You'll have to use the last of your water supply—but sip it. Don't gulp it down or you may vomit and end up even more dehydrated.

↑ *If you have any fruit, suck out the juice. Don't eat anything salty.*

A soldier named Brian K. Fox was trekking across the blisteringly hot Mojave Desert when he realized he'd forgotten his water supply. Soon he was weak and thirsty, so he made a shelter and waited for help. By the time he was rescued, he was severely dehydrated. He had learned his lesson: always carry water!

REAL LIFE SURVIVAL

FIND WATER

You're in the shade and feeling cooler, but your water is finished and you need to find more. Wait until early evening when the sun is less fierce, then start your search.

THINK SMART

Head toward patches of green vegetation as there may be a water source nearby. Watch the sky for birds; they often circle above water, especially at dusk. Animal tracks may also lead to drinking spots such as water holes.

↟ *Walking in the direction of distant green trees could lead to a fantastic sight like this!*

BEWARE!

If you find a water hole, inspect it closely. Is it smelly and **stagnant**? Are there any dead animals in the water? If so, then it contains harmful **bacteria** and will probably make you ill.

➲ *Predators lie in wait at water holes to catch an easy meal. Make sure it isn't you.*

GO WITH THE FLOW

Bacteria can't multiply so well in flowing water, so the best water source is a clear, fast-moving river or stream. Sea water contains salt which will dehydrate you, so avoid it—or remove the salt (see page 21).

↻ *Collect water as far upstream as possible; it will be less polluted.*

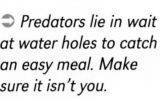

REAL LIFE SURVIVAL

In 2006, Ricky Megee's car was stolen in the Australian **outback**, *leaving him stranded. He walked for days, getting weaker and weaker, until he had a stroke of luck—he came to a lake. He stayed there for weeks, drinking the water and eating raw lizards and frogs, until a farmer found him.*

GET DIGGING

So you've hiked all the way to a promising patch of trees and green grass, only to find a dried-up river bed? Don't despair. You maybe nearer to water than you think!

HIDDEN WATER

If grass and trees are still growing, they must be finding water somewhere. This is likely to be under the ground. Now all you need to do is get to it.

There must be water below this dry river bed to keep the bushes alive.

DIGGING TOOLS

If you packed a good survival kit, then you'll have a small folding shovel. If not, find a long, thick stick to break up the ground, plus a flat rock (or container from your backpack) to scoop out loose soil.

WHAT TO DO

Take your digging tools to the lowest part of the dry river bed. Try to find an area of soil that looks slightly darker and damper. Dig as deep as you can.

REAL LIFE SURVIVAL

Thani Ali Belaisha Al Falasi lived in the desert near Dubai. He was skilled at digging for water and once built a well with his bare hands. It took weeks to complete and was a failure as he didn't find water. Undaunted, he began again nearby and this time the well filled up. It became a life-saving water supply for local people for about ten years.

When the soil becomes wet and muddy, hollow out a wide pond with your hands. Keep digging until water rises to fill it. Leave it to settle and clear.

13

COLLECT WATER

If you can't find any obvious water sources, you'll need to collect drinking water some other way. Here are some simple but clever tricks to try.

DEW DROPS

There may not be any rain water to collect in the desert, but there is **dew**—if you get up early enough! Here are three neat ways to collect it.

Dew drops on grass

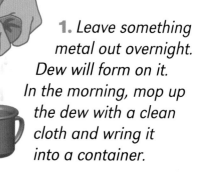

1. *Leave something metal out overnight. Dew will form on it. In the morning, mop up the dew with a clean cloth and wring it into a container.*

2. Dig a shallow pit and spread a piece of polythene on top. Dew will form on the polythene overnight.

3. Tie clean cotton T-shirts or socks around your ankles, then walk through long dewy grass so the cloth soaks up water. Wring them out over a container.

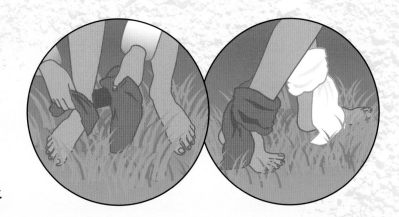

FIND A FROG

Try a method used by Australian Aborigines and drink from a frog! Water-holding frogs store about a cupful of water under a special skin and burrow underground to keep cool. Aborigines dig them up, squeeze them gently so water drips out, then release the frogs unharmed.

Elephant dung

DRINK FROM DUNG

Look out for elephants in the African savannah and squeeze a lump of their dung. It contains a surprising amount of water! You may need to be pretty desperate for a drink before trying this one.

LOOK FOR PLANTS

Many plants in hot places are designed to store water in thick leaves, stems or roots, so cut into them and share their liquid. Let's just hope you remembered to bring a knife.

CUT INTO CACTI

Don't slice up any plant—some are poisonous. Look for barrel cacti like these.

1. *Carefully cut off the top of the cactus and scoop out the pulp. Watch out for sharp spines.*

Barrel cacti

2. *The pulp isn't edible, so wrap it in thin fabric and squeeze out the juice.*

OUTBACK TREES

In Australia, you can dig up the roots of water trees and blood woods, crush them and strain the juice through a cloth. Look for desert oaks, which hold water in their trunk. Aborigines find ant holes in the tree and suck out water through a hollow reed.

Desert oak

REAL LIFE SURVIVAL

John F. Campbell, Jnr. was backpacking with friends in the scorching Guadalupe Mountains, Texas, when they ran out of water. He used his knife to cut off a few sharp-tipped leaves of a yucca plant, then squeezed out enough moisture to keep everyone hydrated and able to trek back to camp.

DRINK SOME JUICE

Fruits such as prickly pears, wild **gourds** and saguaro cactus fruit all contain juice. Unripe coconuts are full of nutritious liquid. Birch trees contain edible **sap** that you can boil to make a sticky syrup.

Prickly pears

Coconut

CLEAN WATER

Drinking any water from the wild is risky. Even if it looks clear, dangerous bacteria may lurk in it. If you can, clean it first. Getting sick in the wilderness is no fun!

TAKE A TABLET

Maybe you've packed water **purification** tablets in your backpack. Good job! Add these to water to kill off nasty bacteria. The water will taste a little odd, but it will be clean.

⮑ *Your hands may be dirty. Wash them before scooping up a drink!*

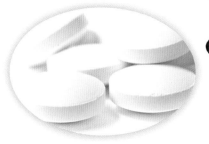

⮑ *Water purification tablets*

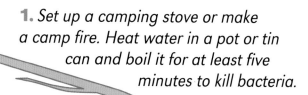

BOIL IT UP

If you didn't bring a cleaning kit, there's another simple but effective method of killing bugs in water: boiling.

1. Set up a camping stove or make a camp fire. Heat water in a pot or tin can and boil it for at least five minutes to kill bacteria.

High in the mountains, water boils at a lower temperature—so keep it bubbling a few minutes longer.

2. Let the water cool before drinking it. It may taste a bit stale, so pour it from cup to cup or blow through it with a straw to freshen it up.

 Boil plenty of water so you can drink some now and save the rest.

In 1585, a French explorer named Jacques Cartier spent the winter stranded near Quebec, Canada. The local **Iroquois** people showed him how to stay healthy by boiling water with pine needles. Boiling made the water safe and the pine needles were full of **vitamin C**.

REAL
LIFE
SURVIVAL

FILTER WATER

ater collected from the wild is likely to be murky, with mud, twigs or insects floating in it. But you don't have to grit your teeth and gulp it down—you can get rid of the particles instead.

USE A PUMP

If you're an experienced explorer, you may have a portable filter pump. These suck water through a tube and strain it to remove bits. The best pumps remove harmful bacteria, too.

Pumps like these filter water into a bottle, ready to drink.

Special filter straws let you drink water straight from the ground.

MAKE YOUR OWN

Here's how to make your own simple filter. Don't forget to boil the water afterwards!

1. *Find a (clean) sock and fill it with fine sand.*

2. *Hang or hold the sock over a container and pour in the water. The water will drain through, leaving any particles trapped in the sand.*

It's easier to pour the water if you stretch out the top of the sock with a frame of twigs and hang it from a tripod of sticks.

*Sailor Steve Callahan drifted on a life raft for 76 days after his boat sank near the Canary Islands. Fortunately he had a small **solar still**, which removes salt from sea water. Having pure water to drink saved his life.*

REAL LIFE SURVIVAL

REMOVE SALT

Here's how to remove salt from sea water. Be careful: steam is very hot.

1. *Heat water in a container over a fire. Cover it with a clean cloth to catch steam.*

2. *Wring the cloth over another container. Cooled, this water will be ready to drink.*

GLOSSARY

bacteria
Tiny, single-celled living things. Some bacteria are harmless; others cause diseases.

dehydrated
Suffering from losing too much water from your body, so it can't function properly.

dew
Water in the air that has cooled and condensed (changed back to liquid) on cool surfaces. This happens at night when the temperature drops. Deserts can get very cold at night!

gourd
A large, tough-skinned fruit, similar to a pumpkin or squash.

heatstroke
An extreme condition in which your temperature becomes so high that your body can't work properly.

Iroquois
A member of a group of Native North American people.

outback
The vast, dry wilderness that covers large parts of Australia.

purification
The process of getting rid of dirt and making something pure.

sap
The liquid inside a plant or tree.

solar still
A device that lets sea water evaporate (turn to gas) in the sun. The water then cools again and turns back to droplets, but with the salt removed.

stagnant
Still, not flowing and fresh.

vitamin C
A healthy substance found in fresh fruits, vegetables and other food. Vitamin C prevents you from getting a painful disease called scurvy.

www.wildwoodsurvival.com/survival/water/index.html
More water facts and tips, including a list of plants containing water.

www.wideworldmag.com/2010/08/11/real-life-desert-survival-stories
Extreme survival tales from the desert.

www.thesurvivalexpert.co.uk/FoodAndWaterCategory.html
All kinds of useful information about finding and cleaning water.

INDEX

animals 8, 11, 15
animal tracks 10
ant holes 17

bacteria 11, 18, 20, 22
birds 10
body temperature 7, 9
boiling 18, 19, 21
breathing 6, 7, 9
bushes 8, 12

cacti 16, 17
caves 8
coconuts 17

dehydration 6, 7, 8, 9, 11, 22
desert oaks 17
dew 14, 15, 22
dung 15

fires 18, 21
frogs 15
frost 15
fruit 9, 17

gourds 17, 22
grass 12, 14, 15

heat exhaustion 7, 8
heatstroke 7, 22

pine needles 19
predators 11
prickly pears 17

river beds 12, 13
rivers 11
roots 16, 17

salt 9, 11, 21
sap 17, 22
sea water 11, 21
shade 8, 10
streams 11
sun 4, 8, 10
sweating 4, 6, 7, 9

trees 8, 10, 12, 17

water filters 20, 21
water holes 10, 11
water purification 18, 19, 22
water sources 10, 11, 12, 13

24

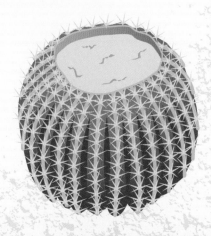